DIARY OF SARAH GILLESPIE

A PIONEER FARM GIRL

by Sarah Gillespie

CAPSTONE PRESS
a capstone imprint

Fact Finders are published by Capstone Press,
1710 Roe Crest Drive, North Mankato, Minnesota 56003
www.capstonepub.com

Library of Congress Cataloging-in-Publication Data
Huftalen, Sarah Gillespie, 1865–1955.
Diary of Sarah Gillespie : a pioneer farm girl / by Sarah Gillespie.
pages cm.—(Fact finders. First-person histories)
Summary: "Presents excerpts from the diary of Sarah Gillespie, a pioneer girl living in Iowa in the late
1860s"—Provided by publisher.
Includes bibliographical references and index.
ISBN 978-1-4765-4194-5 (library binding)
ISBN 978-1-4765-5137-1 (paperback)
ISBN 978-1-4765-5986-5 (ebook PDF)
1. Huftalen, Sarah Gillespie, 1865-1955—Diaries—Juvenile literature. 2. Girls—Iowa—Manchester
Region—Diaries—Juvenile literature. 3. Manchester Region (Iowa)—Biography—Juvenile literature.
4. Manchester Region (Iowa)—Social life and customs—Juvenile literature. 5. Farm life—Iowa—
Manchester Region—Juvenile literature. I. Title.
 F629.M28H84 2014
 977.7'385—dc23   2013027679

Editorial Credits
Carrie Sheely, editor; Bobbie Nuytten, designer; Wanda Winch, media researcher; Laura Manthe,
production specialist

Photo Credits
Alamy: Muskopf Photography, LLC, 26 (top); Bridgeman Art Library: Peter Newark American Pictures/
Private Collection, 22; Corbis:Bettmann, 5, 8, 10, Hulton-Deutsch Collection, 25; Courtesy of Ian Gilman,
cover, 1 (girl); CriaImages.com: Jay Robert Nash Collection, 15; Mary Evans Picture Library, 19; North
Wind Picture Archives, 21, 24; Shutterstock: aarrows, 11, Andrzej Sowa, cover (vintage frames, paper,
left), E.O. 14, Eric Isselée, 20, Glenn Price, 6, Hayati Kayhan, 27, Katya Ulitina, cover (handwriting
background), koka55, 26 (bottom), Picsfive, (ripped paper design element); State Historical Society of
Iowa, Des Moines, 9, State Historical Society of Iowa, Iowa City, Sarah Gillespie Huftalen Collection, cover
(photo Walker, Iowa), 4, 7, 12 (all), 29, Wortman Collection, 16-17; www.largecents.net, 13

Printed in the United States of America.
010694R

TABLE OF CONTENTS

A Difficult Life on the Farm

Sarah Gillespie was born in Manchester, Iowa, on July 7, 1865. Sarah's parents, Emily and James Gillespie, owned a 100-acre (40-hectare) farm in Iowa.

When pioneer farm families like the Gillespies settled across the western United States, much of the land was still wilderness. Pioneers led difficult lives. Some families who came from big cities in the East had never farmed before. Harsh winters, rainy springs, and dry summers made planting and harvesting crops difficult. Few pioneer farm families were able to save money.

Children were expected to help on pioneer farms. Girls helped sew clothes and cook meals. Boys helped care for livestock and repair farm equipment.

Sarah Gillespie, 1888

In her diary Sarah wrote about her life as a pioneer farm girl. She told about the experiences and hardships her family faced. Her diary describes what life was like for many pioneer farm families.

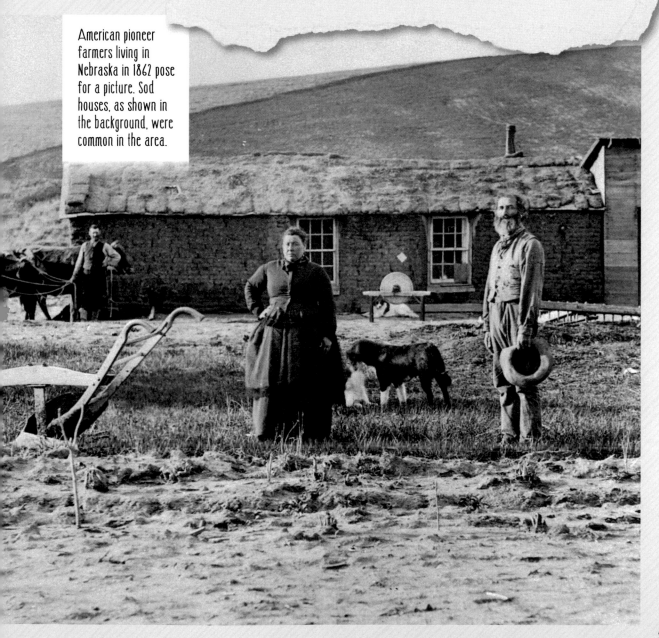

American pioneer farmers living in Nebraska in 1862 pose for a picture. Sod houses, as shown in the background, were common in the area.

THE Diary OF Sarah Gillespie

1877–1878

January 1, 1877 –

New years. I commence to keep a journal to day. Sarah L. Gillespie …

January 3 –

It was so cold we could not go to school. making a whip stalk [**whipstock**]. Henry, Pa, and I took some hay down to Uncle Jerome's and saw the new bridge. It is a very nice one and rests on bars of iron. I got a spool of black thread for me … Ma worked on her Sofa cushion. Warmer.

January 16 –

… I washed all of the dishes, got supper & dinner & made a first-rate jonnie cake [johnnycake]. Cold & Snow.

Sarah's diary entries appear word for word as they were written whenever possible. Because the diary appears in its original form, you will notice misspellings and mistakes in grammar. To make Sarah's meaning clear, in some instances corrections or explanations within a set of brackets follow the mistakes.

Johnnycakes are flat cakes made of cornmeal. The small cakes were a popular food for pioneers. Pioneers often stored them in their saddlebags as they traveled on horseback. For this reason, they were sometimes called journey cakes.

January 22 –

We are not going to School any more it is so lonesome up there with only 4 or 5 **scholars**. Ma worked, she has got a very sore toe, we are going to study at home the rest of the winter. ma says as soon as we get through this **arithmetic** she will get us another one. Pleasant but Cold.

February 14 –

To day is St. Valentines day. I did not send any Valentines nor did not get any. To day was the last day of our school. there were a good many there … Ma did not go.

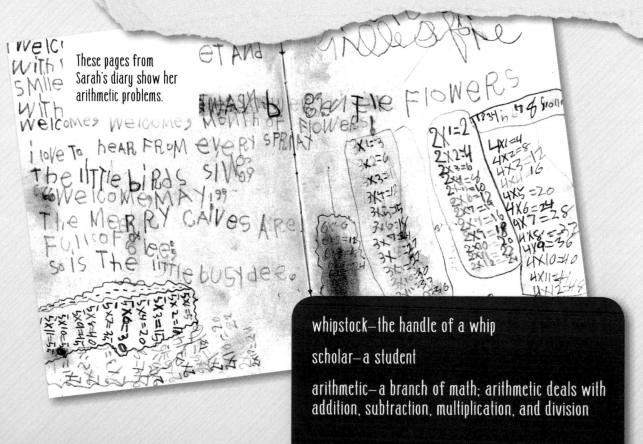

These pages from Sarah's diary show her arithmetic problems.

whipstock—the handle of a whip

scholar—a student

arithmetic—a branch of math; arithmetic deals with addition, subtraction, multiplication, and division

April 3 –

I done 24 **examples** to day. Henry done 19, we go to town, it is very muddy. Sunday evening Barrs livery Stable, the Agricultural Depot & the **Blacksmith** shop was <u>burned</u>. they saved all of the horses but none of the carriages … Mud, Mud, Mud.

Most buildings were made of wood in the 1800s. A fire burning a wooden building was hard to control. Pioneers in rural areas fought fires together. They often formed a single-file line. The people in the back of the line passed water buckets to those in the front.

April 17–

go to school we had 12 scholars, the boys act real mean. the teacher said that there was not 1 boy in the whole school that tended to his own business. Warm.

July 7–

To day I am 12 years old. Warm.

July 28 –

Went up to Uncles get some butter … I have been sick with the belly-ache … Very warm.

Blacksmiths work in their shop around 1880.

Bear Creek township school, Brooklyn, Iowa, 1873

One-Room Schoolhouses

Many children in rural communities attended one-room schoolhouses in the 1800s and early 1900s. Students from farm families often attended school only during the summer and winter months. They helped with chores on the farm during the spring planting and the fall harvest.

Most one-room schoolhouses were small and plain. Children sat on hard benches. A teacher's desk and a blackboard were located at the front of the room.

Each schoolhouse had one teacher. The teacher divided students into groups by their age. Teachers taught reading, writing, math, geography, and history every day. Some teachers also taught art and music once or twice a week.

Children were expected to behave. Teachers sometimes punished children who misbehaved by slapping their hands with a ruler or hitting them on the hand with a thin tree branch.

example—an arithmetic problem

blacksmith—a person who makes and fixes things made of iron, such as horseshoes

August 6 –

Help ma & pa pull weeds in the strawberry patch. I just touched a little young Bird in the nest & all the rest jumped out. I am so sorry. If it would do any good I'd cry. Cool.

September 18 –

Go to school. Ma has been married 15 years to day. We have a surprise party here this evening there were 23 in all ... they presented ma & pa with a set of glass dishes a real nice time we had. moonlight evenings now. Warmer.

Sarah ends almost every diary entry with a comment about the weather. Pioneer farm families were very concerned with the weather. They often tried to predict weather conditions. They could then figure out the best time to plant and harvest crops.

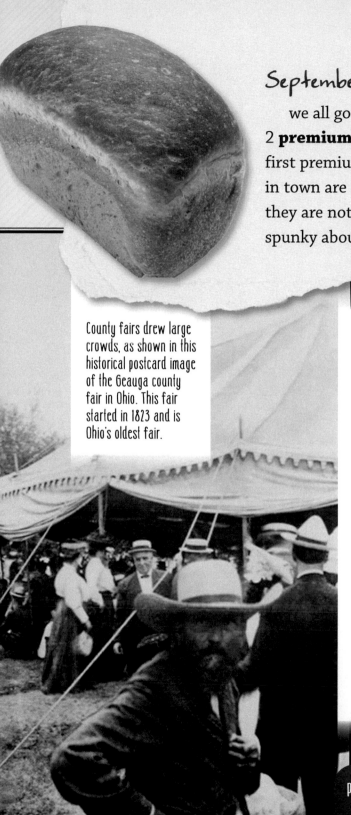

September 27 –

we all go to the fair. we had a good time. I got 2 **premiums** 1 on cake & 1 on bread. Ma has the first premium on a great many things but a few in town are trying to make a fuss about it & say they are not worthy of a premium. ma is a little spunky about it. Foggy.

County fairs drew large crowds, as shown in this historical postcard image of the Geauga county fair in Ohio. This fair started in 1823 and is Ohio's oldest fair.

Going to Fairs

Fairs were a time for pioneers to enjoy themselves and take a break from work. Fairs were usually held once each year. Farmers brought their livestock, crops, and farm equipment to the fair. They entered their goods in competitions with other farmers. Judges awarded premiums to the best entries in each category. Farmers also sold some of their goods and learned about new farming methods at fairs.

Women and children had their own competitions. They entered homemade items such as cakes, breads, canned goods, needlework, and clothing to be judged.

premium—a prize, such as a ribbon or money

December 25 —

got a <u>motto</u> on CardBoard & a pair of slippers, but the slippers were too small, ma is going to exchange them. Henry got a purse pair of clippers & **perforated** motto. Ma got pa a book "The Royal Path of Life," & ma got herself a **morocco** pair worth 2.00. they were very nice & a perforated board motto. We [Sarah and Henry] got a small Christmas tree (A limb of our plum tree) & we hung the presents on it, it looked quite nice. so we did not hang up our stockings. work on my Motto. "What is a home without a mother?" foggy, Rainy.

December 31 —

To day we bid good bye to our old year & wish that our journal will be filled with pleasant & bright hopes ... Colder.

Sarah's parents, James and Emily Gillespie, 1873

Sarah and her brother Henry, 1873

Mottoes were popular in the 1800s. These short sayings usually expressed positive thoughts. Mottoes were often sewn using cloth or painted onto paper.

Cholera is a deadly bacterial disease that people and animals can get. But in hogs, the term cholera is sometimes used to describe the viral disease called classical swine fever.

April 18 –

got our lessons. Pa go to town, get a letter from Mrs. Wood wanting me to learn a piece to speak next Sunday. Easter we are to have kind of **Exhibition** get some herring, hog <u>Cholera</u> Medicine, the papers, and a 10 cent piece changed into pennies for ma get caught in a rain storm ... I took off my hat & then my Apron & covered up so as to keep dry, just as I got home it began to just pour down & then hail ... If I had not run about ¾ of the way I would have got soaked through & through ... Rain.

perforated–having a hole or pattern made by piercing

morocco–a fine leather from goatskin tanned with sumac

exhibition–a public showing

May 3 –

get lessons. our nice little colty [**colt**] died. pa cried. Betsy [the Gillespies' horse] felt very bad. we are all so sorry. Warm

Forgot to say all our little goslings were taken this morning very sudden. pa said they were just going down to the **slough** & all of a sudden the old goose flew up in the cow yard & made a great fuss. pa looked out of the stable but didn't think much about it, until we looked & looked & looked again, but could not find them. too bad. Henry & I went up to Morses to see their little wolves … Warm.

May 22 –

did not get lessons. help pa build a fence. We all go to aunt Hatties & see their nice baby & to uncles. while we were gone 13 of our nicest little turkeys smothered to death. ma felt so sorry about it. ma put an extra quilt over them & fastened with a stick. something she had never done before. Cloudy.

colt–a young male horse

slough–a ditch filled with deep mud

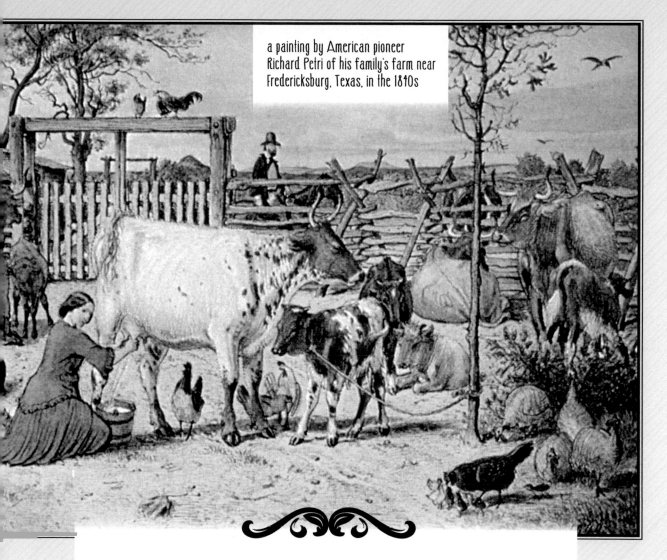

a painting by American pioneer Richard Petri of his family's farm near Fredericksburg, Texas, in the 1840s

Farm Animals

Pioneer farm families owned a variety of farm animals. Some of these animals, such as horses, oxen, and mules, helped with the farmwork. Farm families also raised many animals for food. Cattle were a valuable source of meat. Cow's milk was used to make butter, cream, and cheese. Pigs provided families with bacon, ham, and lard. Families raised sheep for their wool as well as food. Pioneers spun the wool into yarn to make clothing.

Carriages were a common sight on U.S. streets by the late 1800s. This image shows a street in Shenandoah, Iowa.

June 3 –

I am so sorry. those poor old Robins sit on the fence & cry for their little ones, which we think were killed in the hard rain. ma said in the night she thought she heard her turkeys but it must have been those poor little robins. I climbed the tree & ever [every] one was gone. I think it is too bad, did not get lessons. Rain.

June 10 –

I forgot to say that 1 of our little ducks got lost some where & we could not find it. I think that it either got stung & it ran in under some of the shrubbery, or has got on its back & cannot get up. We are so sorry. That was yesterday. I mean (on sunday). it is too bad. help ma & etc. Get lessons. Cold.

June 22 —

get part of lessons. help ma. I am tired ma is ironing & I cannot write very good. Henry go fishing. Quite warm. I forgot to say that pa fell out of the <u>Carriage</u> & hurt his head.

By the late 1880s, horse-drawn carriages were a widely used type of transportation. Families owned small carriages. Larger carriages held several people. These carriages provided a type of public transportation in cities. Accidents were sometimes caused by crashes, runaway horses, or carriage breakdowns.

July 7 –

I am 13 years old to day. go to **Sabbath** school wear my new Pink Chambree dress. in the evening we all take a ride ... this is the way I have celebrated my 13th birthday. Very warm.

July 31 –

To day is the last day of July. I help ma ... just as we got the turkeys & ducks in under some boards & in a box it began to hail & rain.

I tell you it rained so hard that we could hear it over two miles [3 kilometers]. pa said if it was a tornado that we must go down [to the] cellar. it is blowing real hard & raining now. Rain.

August 8 –

go blackberrying. [collecting blackberries] A wolf caught one of the little lambs but he had to let go of it & pa caught & carried the little lamb down here. he was sure that it would die but we (ma & [Henry] & I) got him & put some tar on every place that it was bitten ... the worst places were very near the throat & on the eyelid. we tried to feed it some milk. When the sheep came in the yard we carried it out & it found its mother & tried to eat but he acted as if it hurt him & he is so very weak too by losing so much blood. but I guess that he will get well. I hope so anyhow. go to town and [get] a chance to ride both ways. Warm.

> Pine tar is a sticky substance made from pine trees. It has been used to treat wounds for hundreds of years. It is said to prevent bacterial infection and speed the healing process.

Sabbath–Sunday

Children wore their most formal clothes to Sunday school each week.

September 4 –

Henry is 15 years old to day & Ma make a jelly cake & a common cake & put candles on.

the motto was this: "When first I saw your face so fair; my heart was filled with anxious care." I think it was very good.

September 24 –

[Ma] help me make a necklace to take to the fair. a flea has got onto me & I am just covered in blotches & they itch so I cannot hardly stand it. A wolf came right down to the slough & caught a sheep & I saw the wolf jerk the sheep until he got it down & then we hollowed [hollered] & made just all the noise we could & he left it but he stopped every 2 or 3 **rods** & look around as if he were very much disappointed. Henry go a fishing. I help pa sort out sheep & lambs to take to fair …

rod—a unit of length equal to 16.5 feet (5 meters)

Wolves were numerous in the American wilderness. They were a constant threat to pioneers' livestock.

September 27 –

We all go to fair have a good time ... get the 2nd premium on my handkerchief & on my straw-work ... ma got quite a no. [number] of Red & blue Cards. we entered Betsy in the wrong class or else we would have got the Red Card = $6.00. we entered her as a horse of all work & it ought to have been **draft-horse's** because she is so slow. Pleasant.

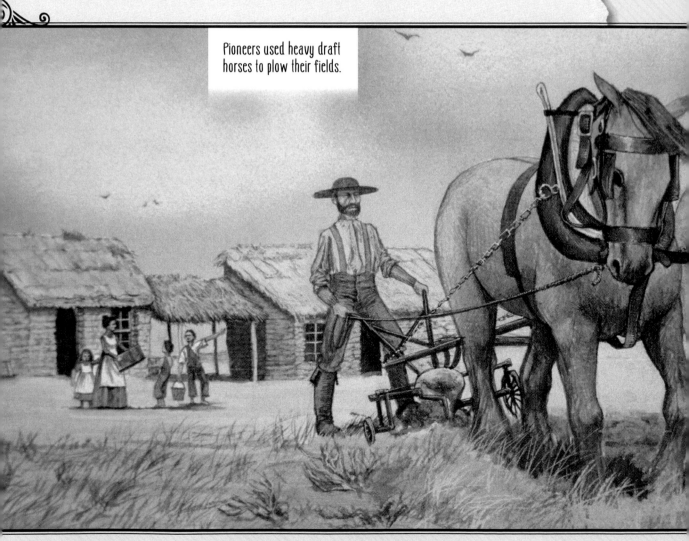

Pioneers used heavy draft horses to plow their fields.

October 5 —

A wolf caught another lamb he caught it in the left side & tore the skin off in a very large place as large as Pas hand ... The butcher would not buy so they [Sarah's parents] brought it back ...

Ma put the skin that was torn down back in place & sewed the wool together then she sewed 2 thicknesses of cloth over it and sewed it to the wool ... I hope it will get well.

Henry took the sheep up above the railroad & watched them for 2 hour's ... I done the morning work .... Help ma. Warm.

draft horse—a tall, heavy horse often used to pull heavy loads

Thanksgiving was a time for pioneers to gather together.

October 27 –

we all go up to Aunt Hatties, she cried because she was so glad that we came. I believe that she & John will separate. he wants to go to Nevada & she will not go & if he goes she says she will never live with him again ... Chilly.

November 28 –

... we had part of a baked pig for thanks-giving dinner ... it was a very beautiful day just like summer. Beautiful.

Thanksgiving became a national American holiday in 1863. like modern-day Americans, pioneers celebrated Thanksgiving with a large meal. Eating wild turkey on Thanksgiving was common by the 1870s. However, the practice wasn't always followed. like today, pioneers gathered with their families on Thanksgiving.

Visiting and Helping Neighbors

Pioneers led very simple lives. They spent a great deal of time farming and doing chores. In the little free time they had, families often visited one another. To make these visits, they sometimes traveled several miles.

Pioneers also helped one another on a daily basis. They helped new settlers build their houses and barns. Pioneer farmers helped one another bring in crops at harvest time. Families who had extra food shared it with their less fortunate neighbors. It was not uncommon for a family who butchered a cow to send some of the best steaks to their neighbor's house.

Farmers use a reaper (being pulled by horses) to harvest grain in the 1870s. This machine made harvesting grain easier. However, pioneer farmers still relied heavily on manual labor.

A re-created building from the 1800s shows some items pioneers had available to them.

December 25 —

Christmas. Go up to Uncles ... we had a good time. I got a Cocoanut, China candle-stick, wax candle (red), A yard of satin Ribbon & some crackers. Santa Claus was very good this time. Henry got the same. Cool.

December 31 —

to day is the last day of the year. go to town get 10 cents worth of paper & 10 cents worth of envelopes & 3 cents worth of candy & a 10 ct salt cellar.

I gave Henry and [Ma] each 6 sheets of **foolscap** & 6 envelopes for New Years, & Divided the candy equal. Get a ride both ways. Warmer.

good bye old year I am ready for the new. Amen. I hope I will have as pleasant a time in 1879 as I had in 1878.

foolscap—a piece of writing paper

27

Preserving Pieces of History

At age 17 Sarah began a teaching career that lasted 54 years. Her first teaching job was at a one-room school not far from Manchester, Iowa. In September 1892 Sarah married William H. Huftalen. Sarah continued teaching in different schools throughout the area until 1935.

Later in life Sarah moved back to the family farm. She collected and organized family letters, photographs, and diaries. Sarah died on February 11, 1955. Before she died, Sarah sent her families' letters, diaries, and other keepsakes to the State Historical Society of Iowa. She wanted others to know about the challenges early pioneers faced. Through her work Sarah helped an important part of American history live on.

Timeline

■ Dates in Sarah Gillespie's life
☐ Important dates in U.S. history

1877
Sarah begins her diary.

1892
Sarah marries William (Billie) Henry Huftalen.

1865
Sarah Gillespie is born.

1861
The Northern states and the Southern states begin to fight the Civil War (1861-1865).

1881
Sarah begins her career as a teacher.

—1860

1890—

1941

Japanese forces bomb Pearl Harbor in the Hawaiian islands. The United States enters World War II (1939-1945).

1919

The 19th amendment to the U.S. Constitution gives women the right to vote.

1952

Sarah donates her family's collection of letters, photographs, and diaries to the State Historical Society of Iowa.

Sarah Gillespie grading papers for students in 1931.

1910

Sarah establishes the rural unit of the Iowa State Teachers Association.

1935

Sarah retires from teaching.

1955

Sarah dies on February 11.

1952

The U.S. Supreme Court orders the end of school segregation.

1910

1950

Glossary

arithmetic (uh-RITH-muh-tik)—a branch of math; arithmetic deals with addition, subtraction, multiplication, and division

blacksmith (BLAK-smith)—a person who makes and fixes things made of iron, such as horseshoes

colt (KOHLT)—a young male horse

draft horse (DRAFT HORS)—a tall, heavy horse often used to pull heavy loads

example (ig-ZAM-puhl)—an arithmetic problem

exhibition (ek-suh-BI-shuhn)—a display that usually includes objects and information to show and tell people about a subject

foolscap (FULZ-kap)—a piece of writing paper

morocco (muh-RAH-koh)—a fine leather from goatskin tanned with sumac

perforated (PUR-fuh-rayt-uhd)—having a hole or pattern made by piercing

pioneer (pye-uh-NEER)—a person who is among the first to settle in a new land

premium (PREE-mee-uhm)—a prize or reward

rod (ROD)—a unit of length equal to 16.5 feet (5 meters)

Sabbath (SAB-uhth)—Sunday

scholar (SKOL-ur)—a student

slough (SLOO)—a ditch filled with deep mud

whipstock (WIP-stok)—the handle of a whip

Read More

Bliss, John. *Pioneers to the West.* Children's True Stories: Migration. Chicago: Raintree, 2012.

Schwartz, Heather E. *The Foul, Filthy American Frontier: The Disgusting Details About the Journey out West.* Disgusting History. Mankato, Minn.: Capstone Press, 2010.

Critical Thinking Using the Common Core

1. Many Americans displayed mottoes in their homes and buildings during the late 1800s. Look at the mottoes shown in the schoolhouse image on page 9. What do you think these mottoes mean or are meant to inspire? What would your motto be? Explain why. (Integration of Knowledge and Ideas)

2. Look at the costs of items on page 27. What do these costs tell you about how much money people earned or had then? Use the Internet or print advertising to find out how much envelopes, paper, candy, and salt shakers cost today. Compare the costs of items then and now. (Craft and Structure)

3. On page 24, Sarah mentions that her aunt cried upon her family's arrival. In what ways do you think the distance between relatives and neighbors affected the way pioneers interacted? (Key Ideas and Details)

Internet Sites

FactHound offers a safe, fun way to find Internet sites related to this book. All of the sites on FactHound have been researched by our staff.

Here's all you do:

Visit *www.facthound.com*

Type in this code: 9781476541945

 Check out projects, games and lots more at **www.capstonekids.com**

Index

Writing Stories
Mystery Stories

Anita Ganeri

Chicago, Illinois

Edited by Dan Nunn, Rebecca Rissman,
and Sian Smith
Designed by Joanna Hinton-Malivoire
Original illustrations © Capstone Global
Library 2013
Picture research by Ruth Blair
Production by Sophia Argyris
Originated by Capstone Global Library Ltd

ISBN: 978 1 4329 7532 6 (Hardback)
ISBN: 978 1 4329 7539 5 (Paperback)

Cataloging-in-Publication Data is available at the
Library of Congress website.
Ganeri, Anita, 1961-
  Mystery stories / Anita Ganeri.
    pages cm.—(Writing Stories)
  Includes bibliographical references and index.
  ISBN 978-1-4329-7532-6 (hb)—ISBN 978-1-4329-
7539-5 (pb) 1. Detective and mystery stories—
Authorship. 2. Creative writing. I. Title.

PN3377.5.D4G36 2013
808.3'872—dc23   2012043115

Acknowledgments
We would like to thank the following for permission
to reproduce photographs: Shutterstock,
background images and design, pp.4 (© Kamira),
5 (© Zurijeta), 6 (© Fer Gregory), 7 (© Richard
Peterson), 8 & 9 (© Monkey Business Images),
12 (© Chad Zuber), 14 (© alsamua), 16 (© Neda
Sadreddin), 16 & 22 (© HiSunnySky), 24 (©
A.Krotov), 24 (© zhykova), 26 (© Nattika).

Cover photographs reproduced with permission
of istockphoto (© GaryAlvis) and Shutterstock (©
VikaSuh, © Hywit Dimyadi).

Every effort has been made to contact copyright
holders of material reproduced in this book. Any
omissions will be rectified in subsequent printings if
notice is given to the publisher.

All the Internet addresses (URLs) given in this book
were valid at the time of going to press. However,
due to the dynamic nature of the Internet, some
addresses may have changed, or sites may have
changed or ceased to exist since publication. While
the author and publisher regret any inconvenience
this may cause readers, no responsibility for any
such changes can be accepted by either the author
or the publisher.

Some words are shown in bold, **like this**. You can find out what they mean by looking in the glossary.

Contents

Follow this symbol to read a mystery story.

What Is a Story?

A story is a piece of **fiction** writing. It describes made-up people, places, and events. Before you start writing your story, you need to figure out a **setting**, **characters**, and a **plot**.

There are lots of different types of stories. You can write scary stories, funny stories, fairy tales, adventure stories, animal stories, and lots more. This book is about writing mystery stories.

Mystery Stories

A mystery story needs an exciting mystery to solve, someone to **investigate** the mystery, clues, and **suspects**. When you start writing, you should know how the mystery is solved, but make sure you do not give it away too soon.

Sherlock Holmes is a detective who stars in a series of mystery stories written by Arthur Conan Doyle. The stories are set in London, England, about 100 years ago. Holmes is famous for solving mysteries that no one else can solve.

Story Ideas

Get some ideas for your story before you start writing. Look in books, on the Internet, on TV, or use your imagination. You should also read lots of mystery stories by other writers. This can help to spark ideas.

Jot down your ideas in a notebook so that you do not forget them. Then you can look at them when you start writing. Always keep your notebook handy, even at night. You never know when an amazing idea will come.

What Happens Next?

What happens in your mystery story? This is called the **plot**. The plot needs a beginning, a middle, and an end. You can try using a **story mountain**, like the one below, to help you figure out your plot.

Middle
The main action happens. There may be a problem for one of your characters.

Beginning
Set the scene and introduce your main **characters**.

Ending
The problem is solved and the story ends.

Your story starts at one side of the mountain, goes up to the top, then goes down the other side.

When you are planning your plot, you need to put events in the right order. You can use a **timeline** to help you. Here is a timeline for the mystery story in this book.

Mom finds the cookie jar empty.

⬇

She searches the kitchen.

⬇

Mom asks Dad and Harry if they ate the cookies.

⬇

Harry starts trying to solve the mystery.

⬇

Harry looks for clues.

⬇

Harry interviews the main **suspects.**

⬇

Harry lays a trap to catch the thief.

⬇

The cookie thief is caught.

In the Beginning

The beginning of your story is where something happens to get your story started. It should grab your readers' attention and make them want to keep reading. It is also where you introduce your main **characters**.

"That's strange," thought Mom, peering into the cookie jar. "It's empty."

The start of your story should draw your readers in.

A Mystery Story

"That's strange," thought Mom, peering into the cookie jar. "The jar is empty."

She turned it upside down, just to make sure.

"I'm sure that I filled it up yesterday," she thought. "Dad and Harry can't have eaten them all!"

Can you think of another way to start this story?

Crime Scene

The **setting** is the place and time in which your story happens. You can set a mystery story somewhere dramatic, such as in a deep, dark forest or in an old, creaky hotel. You can also set it somewhere ordinary, such as at school or at home.

In a mystery story, the setting may also be a **crime scene**.

Mom looked around the kitchen. Everything else seemed to be in the right place. She looked in all the cabinets. She searched on all the shelves. She looked in the refrigerator. She looked in the dog's bowl. But she couldn't find the missing cookies anywhere.

 Add more details to the description to bring your setting to life.

15

Character Files

Creating strong **characters** is very important. You want your readers to care about them and believe in them. Write fact files for your main characters. Think about what the characters look like and how they think, feel, and behave.

Character fact file
Character: Mom
Age: Not saying
Looks like: Short; glasses; long, brown hair
Personality: Kind; a bit forgetful
Likes: Having a cookie with her morning coffee
Dislikes: When the cookies disappear

Character fact file
Character: Harry
Age: 8
Looks like: Medium height; short, brown hair
Personality: Helpful; smart; curious
Likes: Dogs; detective stories
Dislikes: Getting blamed for everything

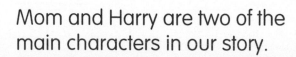

Mom and Harry are two of the main characters in our story.

When Harry got home from school, Mom was waiting with the cookie jar.

"Anything to tell me?" she asked, pointing to the empty jar.

"Maybe you left them somewhere Mom," said Harry. "I mean, you do, um, lose things sometimes."

Mom tried again when Dad got home.

"They're probably in the dog," said Dad. "He always looks hungry."

Ordinary people can make interesting characters, too.

In the Middle

The middle of your story is where the main action happens. This is where your **characters** face a tricky problem or have a mystery to solve. You might have several ideas about what happens next. Here are two possible **plots** for our story.

The cookies have disappeared.

1. Harry tries to solve the mystery.

2. Mom finds the cookies. The dog has buried them in his bed.

Can you think of any other plot ideas?

Suddenly, Harry rushed up to his room. When he came back, he was clutching a magnifying glass and a large notebook.

"Don't worry, Mom," he said. "Detective Harry—and his dog— are here to solve the Mystery of the Missing Cookies."

"Humph," said Dad. "I bet that means you'll want a reward."

Mind Mapping

Even the best writers sometimes get stuck about what to write. If you need help figuring out what happens next, try using a **mind map**. Write down a key word or idea. Then jot down other words or ideas that are connected to it.

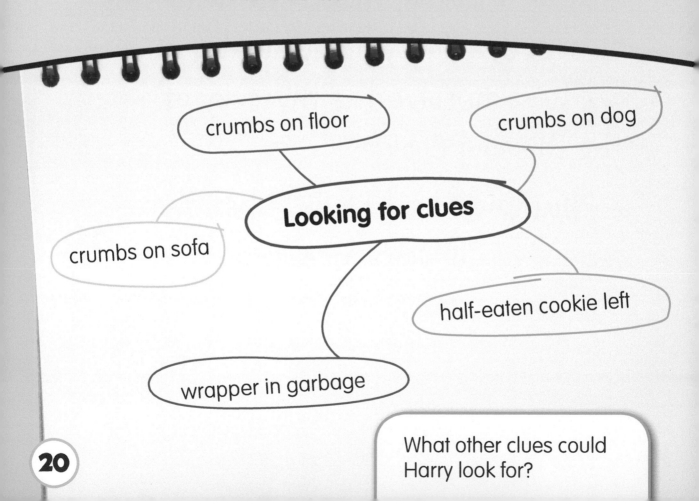

crumbs on floor

crumbs on dog

Looking for clues

crumbs on sofa

half-eaten cookie left

wrapper in garbage

What other clues could Harry look for?

Harry began searching for clues. He didn't have to look very hard. He found cookie crumbs on the hall carpet and on the kitchen floor. There were even cookie crumbs on the dog.

"I wonder what that's doing there?" said Harry, picking up a half-eaten cookie from Dad's bedside table.

You need to keep the story moving on, without giving the answer to the mystery away.

21

Speaking Parts

Dialogue means the words people say. Adding dialogue to your story helps bring it to life and makes your **characters** more believable. Try to think about how each of your characters might sound if they spoke out loud.

"Mom," he said. "How many cookies have you had today?"

Put **quotation marks** around the spoken words.

Next, Harry decided to interview the chief suspects.

"Mom," he said. "How many cookies have you had today?"

"Um, none," said Mom. "That's the problem."

"Dad," said Harry. "Can you explain what this cookie was doing in your bedroom?"

"I have no idea," said Dad. "It is because of that dog. Ask him."

 Dialogue can help your readers to learn more about your characters.

23

Mystery Writing

In a mystery story, it is important to make your writing exciting. Choose your words carefully. For example, you can use lots of different **adjectives**, **adverbs**, and **verbs** to add interesting details to your writing.

That night, after Mom and Dad had gone to bed, Harry <u>sneaked</u> downstairs and set up a <u>cunning</u> trap for the cookie thief.

Sneaked is a verb. *Cunning* is an adjective.

That night, after Mom and Dad had gone to bed, Harry sneaked downstairs and set up a cunning trap for the cookie thief. He put new cookies in the jar and left it on the kitchen table. Then he tied a long piece of string around the jar. He tied the other end around his finger. Finally, Harry went into the family room next door, settled down on the sofa, and fell fast asleep.

Use sentences of different lengths to add interest.

Whodunit?

The ending of your story is where you solve the mystery and tie up any loose ends. Try not to give the ending away earlier in the story. That way, it will come as a surprise to your readers.

Possible endings

Mom had left the cookies in the bathroom.

Dad had been eating the cookies in his sleep.

The dog had buried the cookies in the backyard.

Can you think of any more endings?

A few hours later, Harry felt a tug on his finger. He crept into the kitchen. A shadowy figure was munching a cookie. The cookie thief was... Dad!

"Got you, Dad!" said Harry, but Dad didn't seem to hear him. He was still fast asleep!

"I had a funny dream last night," said Dad, the next morning. Mom and Harry said nothing. They just looked at each other and smiled.

 Use your ending to tell your readers what happens to your **characters**.

More Top Tips

1. Read some mystery stories by other writers. This will help you to improve your own writing and may spark ideas.

2. Don't give away your mystery too soon. It will spoil the ending if the reader knows "whodunit" too early in the story.

3. Keep your readers guessing by having several **suspects**. You can also add some false clues.

4 Always read your story through after you have finished. Spot and correct any mistakes. You may need to do this several times.

5 A mystery story should be exciting. Use short sentences to speed up the **pace** of your writing and add excitement.

?

6 Think of a great title for your story. Choose something that will make people eager to read the story.

Glossary

adjective describing word that tells you about a noun (a noun is a naming word)

adverb describing word that tells you about a verb (a verb is a doing word)

character person in a piece of writing

crime scene place where a crime happens

dialogue words that characters say

fiction writing about made-up things

investigate find out about a mystery or crime

mind map diagram of ideas on a subject

pace speed at which a story moves along

plot what happens in a story

quotation marks marks that show spoken words

setting time and place in which a story is set

story mountain diagram for planning a story

suspect person who could have carried out a crime

timeline list of events and when they happen

verb doing or action word

Find Out More

Books

Ganeri, Anita. *Writing Stories*. Chicago: Raintree, 2013.

Stowell, Louie, and Jane Chisholm. *Write Your Own Story Book*. Tulsa, Okla.: EDC, 2011.

Warren, Celia. *How to Write Stories* (How to Write). Laguna Hills, Calif.: QEB, 2007.

Web sites

Facthound offers a safe, fun way to find Internet sites related to this book. All of the sites on Facthound have been researched by our staff.

Here's all you do:
Visit **www.facthound.com**
Type in this code: 9781432975326.

Index